Travelling with friends

Stephanie Kirby

Published by

MELROSE BOOKS

An Imprint of Melrose Press Limited
St Thomas Place, Ely
Cambridgeshire
CB7 4GG, UK
www.melrosebooks.com

FIRST EDITION

Copyright © Stephanie Kirby 2007

The Author asserts her moral right to
be identified as the author of this work

Cover designed by Tom Brennand

ISBN 978-1-906050-18-4

Printed and bound in Great Britain by:
CPI Bath, Lower Bristol Road,
Bath, BA2 3BL, UK

Introduction

The reason I wanted to write this book was to show that the reality of God's presence in the world today is available to everyone, everywhere. There are a lot of good books about telling how God has rescued people from death, disease, drugs or a life of crime. They are very inspiring but they can seem like a fantasy story, a million miles away from me. There are other books about God that are so intellectual and full of theory that it is hard to apply them to my own life.

I wanted to write a different account about how I try to live with God in my life and I have asked some of my friends to contribute examples of this from their own experiences. We are quite ordinary people and don't make headline news. You would not give us a second glance if you passed us in the street! Although we may feel as if we are each just another grain of sand on the seashore, we know that to God we are special and he is interested in us as unique individuals. From the beginning he has wanted to

communicate with us and I hope to show, through the following pages, how this can happen if we are willing to play our part.

The following chapters will take the form of a journey, which is not an original idea I know. I hope you will travel with me. Along the way we will meet some of my special friends who will provide comfort, direction, and new insights. We will be travelling in new country and learning new ways.

My wish is that after travelling my journey with me and by meeting some of my fellow companions, you will start on the special journey for yourself. If you do, please let me know how you get on.

Chapter One

Preparation for the Journey of a Lifetime

My journey starts with preparation. I have the feeling that this is not the "see where the wind blows me" sort of journey. It's going to take a long time – my lifetime – and I will not be coming back. At all times on my journey I will need to have an inner calm and security as to who I am, to enable me to carry on. I will need to know where I am going even though I have no idea of how to get there and the details of the journey are not clear at all.

So I will begin the journey, not with a flurry of outward activity as you would if preparing for a holiday or special trip, but rather with inward reflection, some decision making and some giving up of old ways of thinking.

I know that the road I will be travelling on has been well trodden. Many people have gone that way before me down the years. The way I must go starts with Jesus. He has said about himself, 'I am the Way, the Truth and the Life; no-one comes to the Father but through me.'

My journey is along that Way. How can I prepare for such a journey?

I have a problem with communicating with God. It doesn't matter how many good books I read, how much study and learning I do, how much I know my subject. I can shout at God, plead with him, bargain with him but it all just seems to fall on deaf ears or disappears into a black hole. I can try and win his favour by being good but I can't keep that up for long and anyway who am I trying to fool? I can read his book from cover to cover and go to church at every available opportunity but still nothing seems to get through and I wonder, is this all there is? Can I really get close to God, and how is it done?

I have come to the conclusion that this is something we cannot do for ourselves. Eventually we all run out of our own resources and have to admit that there are just some things we cannot cope with. This is why God sent Jesus to help us to gain a family relationship with him. Jesus is able to be the link between the two parties, us and God. He was human and so could identify with us in all our weaknesses and fully understand our predicaments but he was also fully God and so was perfect in every way.

From the beginning God had chosen a people, the Jews, to be his own nation on earth, Israel, and had shown them a pattern of how to behave, which is recorded for us in the Bible, in the Old Testament. He had given them laws to follow and ways to approach him for forgiveness when they broke those laws. There were a great many laws because God is absolutely perfect and his justice cannot be compromised. He is light and there is no darkness in him. They were told that if they broke just one of the laws then it was as if they had broken them all. The way back into his forgiveness was by shedding the blood of a perfect unblemished animal in substitution for themselves. They deserved to die, but he would accept the blood of the sacrificed animal instead. Through all of this, God is demonstrating that we cannot by ourselves obtain the state of perfection that is required; we will always fall short. All through the Old Testament God is proclaiming the coming of a Messiah or Saviour who will save God's nation from all its troubles. However, when Jesus was born and then began his ministry everyone was expecting some sort of warrior king and not a humble carpenter. His teaching had authority and he performed many miracles. He gained a great following of disciples but his destiny was to open the way to God by becoming the sacrificial lamb. He was perfect and no wrong was found in him but he was willing to take all our sickness and sins onto himself and be a substitution for us. He was willing to give up his life by being crucified on a cross. His was a once and for all sacrifice. By his blood he has opened the way for all mankind to approach God. The old way has gone and the new way has begun. His teachings and the teachings of his followers are all written down in the New Testament – which means the new way or the new promise.

My preparation for this journey of Christian life must start with me acknowledging my need, turning away from my old life, and accepting Jesus into my life. My preparation involves a complete giving up of my life and rights into the hands of God through Jesus. My soul is stripped bare and my spirit is reborn into a new way of living with Jesus. I can then become part of a new creation, God's kingdom, and have access to all the blessings and power and authority of God himself.

Although I don't know it at the time this is to be the greatest decision I'll ever make. For now I am a new person, the old has gone for ever and the new has come. I have crossed over from darkness to light.

Having made the decision to accept Jesus as the one who has saved me from the old way, Jesus has promised to be with me always. He has also promised to give me the gift of the Holy Spirit who will remind me about God and teach me how to grow in the new life. Where the Spirit is, then there is life and if there is no Spirit then there is no life. Life has now changed and is different in lots of ways.

Before we start I want to take a look at the people we will meet as we travel. As I said before, they are quite an ordinary set of people but extraordinary as well. It is as if they were two people at the same time, but not in the way that people are perceived differently by each person they meet. This is as if they are two different species in the same body. One is human and mortal and is what you can see and touch, the other is "spiritual" and immortal, walking as a child of God in his world at the same time as walking on the earth in humanity (strangers in a strange land). We rely heavily on our senses to make judgements about our world and can therefore often miss the spiritual aspect of a situation. My understanding is that God is spirit and therefore to be alive with God my own spirit needs to be re-kindled by God, which is what Jesus called being born-again. We need to be born into the spiritual world of God's kingdom. I want to make it clear now that I am not talking about spiritualism or getting in touch with spirits of dead people. Being born into God's world is a specific action that can only be done by God through the work of his Holy Spirit.

My friends have all made their commitment to Jesus and as you will see all of them have different stories to tell. God treats us all individually and doesn't have a "one size fits all" attitude to us. It is very personal and initially I found that quite a barrier to cross. There is a certain security in following the "establishment" in that you can detach yourself from any accountability, you can retain some control of your situation and you don't need to think things through or take responsibility – the "Church" can do all that. I think it is sad when people fall for that temptation because they miss out on the wonderful blessings and revelations that are available when you get personal with God. In my view, Jesus paid a huge price for us and it doesn't seem right to throw it back in his face by keeping him at arm's-length, or making him into some sort of stained glass, unapproachable icon, or even by making our own restrictions such as, 'I am not good enough for Jesus', or 'God doesn't want to be bothered with my little life'.

None of these arguments has any credibility when matched up to what God actually says in the bible. He has promised so much. Here is a small example –

1. *that nothing can separate us from his love*

2. *whatever we ask for he will give us*

3. *we will have eternal life*

4. *he will be with us always*

5. *he has promised us hope and a future*

6. *forgiveness and healing*

7. *freedom*

8. *no condemnation*

The bible is full of wonderful promises that God has made as his part of the pledge.

We all have emotional baggage to carry around with us. We have wrong attitudes, misunderstandings, irrational fears, bad experiences and the list goes on. The Father's love for us working in our lives brings us wholeness and healing that we cannot find elsewhere in the world. This needs to be told because there is so much need in the world today. There is a place in us that only God can fill and until that happens there is an emptiness in us and a sense of searching for something better. Until we find God, we search around in the world for happiness and fulfilment. We know it's out there somewhere! Putting aside the very great needs of poverty, infant mortality rates, abuse and war in the world as a whole, in the affluent developed countries young people are self-abusing, committing suicide, drug taking etc, etc. Some groups in our society are increasingly willing to take to expressing their opinions violently with self-approved justifications. Our standard of living may have improved but our society has deep problems.

God wants us to love each other whatever our age, colour, creed, or status. He wants us to be builders, not destroyers. We are not to judge people as worthy or unworthy. God sees into the hearts of people and can see their potential. We should treat everyone we meet as people that are loved by God and give them that due respect.

If we have had an unfortunate brush with organised religion or church we can reject God at the same time as rejecting the church. My early upbringing meant that my impression of God was that he was scary and blamed me for everything. After I was about 12 years old I gave up trying to be perfect and ditched church with all the accompanying fear and guilt. Later on I was fortunate enough to meet people who showed me that he isn't like that and I could meet him for myself and know that it wasn't a correct view. Some of these people have contributed examples for this book. They have had revelations from God that have impacted on their lives and have provided encouragement for themselves and for the building up of others.

The first story is from my friend Alison and is an account of her preparation for her journey with God:

I remember the day clearly; it was May 18th 1993 and I was at a meeting with the team of speech and language therapists that I work with. I had a really sore throat and at the end of the day I turned to my boss and said that I thought I might not be in the next day. That was the last full day I worked for the next 18 months! I didn't recover from the virus that caused the sore throat and was eventually diagnosed with "post viral fatigue syndrome" or ME, as most people know it.

Maybe you know someone who has ME. Each person is different … let me tell you how it affected me. Imagine you've got a really bad dose of flu. You are pinned to the bed, unable to get enough energy to move. Your head aches and all your muscles ache and you just want to sleep all the time. This is like ME but add to that times when:

your heart races for no apparent reason

your brain seems to be in a fog and you can't think straight

sometimes you can't think of the words or complete a sentence you started

the room suddenly seems to spin round and round when you are lying down

the skin on your arms and legs becomes hypersensitive and the touch of material can feel as though you are being scraped with sandpaper

you start off to walk ok but find your legs begin to feel as if you are wading through treacle and you wind down like a clockwork toy you never know from hour to hour how you will feel

and life is on hold and you can't plan ahead

There is no cure for ME ... it is up to individuals to learn to pace themselves very carefully. You take each day as it comes and try to use up only 75% of the energy you have. At first this may only be enough just to crawl to the bathroom and back ... but very gradually over the months and then years, as you learn to pace yourself, most people's energy level increases. There are always relapses when you push yourself too far or catch an infection. This was my life for three years. I gradually did improve to about 60% functioning but never knew when the next bad patch was coming. It wasn't just my life that was affected but my husband Robert too suffered because of it. We had only been married two years when he was suddenly thrust into the role of carer.

One of the things you have lots of with ME is time to think ... when your brain allows you to. About a year in, I reached the point where I could read more than a few pages a day and I began to think and read about spiritual issues ... the meaning of life takes on a new importance when you spend a high percentage of the day flat out on the sofa. I come from a Christian family but was very anti for a long time. My husband Robert was a Christian and I would go to church with him to sing in the choir but the services meant very little. Now, I stopped running away and began to think about it seriously. Two years after the ME began I realised that Jesus really was the son of God and asked him to come into my life.

In April 1996 we went with a group from Christchurch here in Hitchin to Spring Harvest. This is a week-long Christian event where thousands of Christians take over Butlins. There are seminars and huge celebrations where thousands of people from all types of churches worship God and learn together.

The first few days proved to be really frustrating. Everyone in our group was rushing about having a great time. I felt the limitations of my illness and I guess the others in the group saw these for the first time, rather than just seeing me for an hour or so on Sundays. I became more and more tired and was only emerging from the chalet mid-morning. I was having difficulty getting about because you have to walk everywhere at these events and my legs kept giving up … there was even talk of borrowing a wheelchair.

I remember having to sit in an evening celebration (surrounded by hundreds of people standing up and praising God) and bursting into tears with the frustration of it all. A lady approached me and asked if I wanted to be prayed for … this was not something I had ever done … but I agreed … in between sobs. As soon as she started to pray the tears stopped as if someone had turned a tap off. Then this tremendous peace descended on me and I felt as if waves of cool water were flowing over and through me from head to foot. I remember her saying that Jesus understood my suffering and my need for rest.

The next day that peace was still there and I tried to get my brain round what had happened. I went off in the afternoon to two seminars on healing. The second one was a "practical" session and I put up my hand for more prayer. Two friends from church were there with me. One of the prayer team came over and prayed for me. After a while I was aware of this tremendous weight pressing down on me, bending me over as I sat there. This faded and the lady left ... however my two friends continued to pray and the same thing happened over and over again. When we got up to leave I was aware that there seemed to be a core of energy within me that I hadn't had for three years. I went to the book shop and then started back towards the chalet ... I had this urge to run and I did ... all evening the energy just bubbled up. In the celebration that evening I was no longer slumped in my seat or leaning on Robert's arm, I was up on my feet dancing and singing. The next day I was up making breakfast at 7.45 to the complete amazement of the couple we were sharing with. And so it continued ... I was bursting with energy and couldn't keep still for long. It began to dawn on me that this was different to the "good days" I'd sometimes had before ...the real me was back and raring to go ... Praise be to God ... He had healed me.

Over the next few months the muscle aches and other physical symptoms gradually disappeared but the core of energy never faded and is still there now. It took six months to convince my work colleagues that I was completely better but with no days off sick in that time they had to believe me and give me my old job back.

As I look back now on that time, and the miraculous way God healed me, I am overwhelmed with gratitude to Him. But it wasn't just getting physically better that changed my life. ME gave me the chance to get off the treadmill and have time to meet with God. Getting to know Jesus personally as a friend, as well as the one who saved me, has given my life a wholeness that is more than just physical wellbeing. I truly am a new creation as it says in the bible ... and this is there for everyone.

Another example is from Jeremy. He says:

I want to tell you about how and why I started to take God seriously.

I was born in Dublin in 1957 but my family soon moved north, first to Londonderry and then to Bangor, a town 14 miles from Belfast. My father played the organ in various Church of Ireland churches and as a family, we regularly attended Sunday services. Although I was confirmed at the age of 13, by the following year I had had enough of church and quickly drifted away.

After leaving school, I took various jobs in Northern Ireland and latterly in London and met Renate, who was to become my future wife. We were living happily together in a rented house and we began to think seriously about what I wanted to do for a career. I felt drawn to becoming a teacher, so at the age of 24 years I applied to Middlesex Polytechnic and was accepted onto a teaching course.

I had been out of the routine of studying for six years and the first half term was really tough. In late October an earache developed in my left ear. It was the most awful tormenting pain I have ever experienced. The pain seemed to be raging deep inside my head. My doctor could see the inflammation and prescribed very strong painkillers. So great was the pain that the effect of the medication wore off after one hour. Given the strength of the tablets, I was not allowed a repeat dose until four hours had passed. This left three hours of unbearable pain.

This situation carried on for two whole days. By this time, I was desperate.

One of my three brothers had for many years been a "born again Christian". Occasionally, he had tried to talk to me about God but generally I had resisted. I had not enjoyed the church experience of my younger years so my attitude towards religion ranged somewhere between being negative and generally disinterested. I definitely felt very far from God and I was quite content with this situation.

However, in desperation, from the depth of my torment, I spoke to God. I told him that if he took the pain away, I would seriously consider who he was and what he meant to me. I did not really know what would happen or even whether to expect any response. By evening, the pain had subsided. The next morning, painkillers were no longer needed. Within two days I was back at college.

Although I did not know it, one of the members of my college class was also keen on Christianity. Two weeks later he invited me to an evening meeting of the college Christian Union, of which he was already a member. I was not particularly enamoured. As I lived in Harrow, many miles from Barnet, it meant staying late, but as I was still feeling my way at college and trying to be open-minded, I thought I should give it a go.

At the meeting, a guest speaker arrived and the group soon began to sing choruses. I was not impressed. The speaker was introduced and he spoke about the passage in Matthew chapter 7, where Jesus was talking about the wide and the narrow gate. He explained that many people in this world choose the wide straight easy path and try to enter heaven by the wide gate. For them, however, it leads to destruction and hell. I began to sit up and take notice. He then went on to say that only a few people choose to walk the difficult narrow twisting path which Jesus calls us to follow. At the end of this path is the narrow gate which leads to heaven and eternal life. At that moment, I decided from then on I only wanted to walk the narrow path, although I did not really know what that entailed.

When the meeting had ended, I went to talk to the guest speaker. He told me about the church he attended each

Sunday, which was St Helens in the City of London, and suggested I come along to the bible study classes, which were held every Wednesday evening. This was a test for me because it meant travelling into London after a long day at college, attending the bible study class which finished at 10.00pm, and then travelling home to Harrow. However, I started attending regularly and was not disappointed.

Renate and I had been growing closer to the point where we decided we wanted to be married. Things were going well for us and we were looking forward to a bright future together. We decided on a wedding the following summer. I was learning more about the Christian life and what God wanted from me. I understood that I needed to decide whether or not I believed that Jesus had died for my sins and that I was willing to give my life to God. One evening in February, the group leader took me aside and asked, did I want to take that step? Without having to think too hard, I agreed and became a Christian that evening.

Over the following weeks, the implications of what I had chosen to do began to become apparent. Renate had been raised as a Catholic, but had also drifted away from religion and did not consider herself a Christian. Faced with my newly acquired faith, she began to fire questions at me, many of which I found difficult to answer. By now, dark clouds were gathering.

Matters came to a head one evening at a bible study class. The general consensus was that it was not right for a Christian to marry a non-Christian. The choice was clear. Was I going to choose God or Renate? I was also very concerned that if I walked away from her, she would forever hold God to account and perhaps be prevented from becoming a Christian. I prayed long and hard, agonising over the dilemma for several days. I finally told God I was going to do the right thing by Him, irrespective of the consequences. It was the hardest decision I have ever had to make. Renate was my most cherished love to whom I was soon to be married but I was willing to give her up if that was what God required.

Immediately a feeling of peace came over me and I knew God was saying it was okay for me to get married to Renate irrespective of whether she was a Christian or not.

The people at St Helens were dubious. A senior cleric at St Helens even counselled both of us to step back from the brink and reconsider, especially as Renate came from a Catholic background! In July, we were married at the registry office in Harrow and travelled to Germany in July to be married in church in Renate's home village.

After moving to Hitchin, I soon joined a bible study/ prayer group at a local church. Some of the members joined with me in praying over a number of years that Renate would become a Christian. I reached a point one evening where God gave me the assurance that Renate would indeed give her life to Him and from that moment on, I never felt the need to use that prayer again. At least another year went by and one day she smiled at me and told me the good news! This, however, is another story.

Renate and I have been very happily married for over 20 years. I can now look back and see some of God's plan for my life. Although I did not realise it at the time, he laid the foundations during my early life and then provided people around me to pray and to bring me closer to Him. He also has provided all the answers. I have agonised over many issues needlessly, but God has always provided the solutions when I have trusted in Him. Our marriage is one such example and a real blessing to our family.

Chapter Two

First Steps

With my preparation completed, and in such excellent company, I start on my journey of a lifetime. I take nothing with me of my own but put my trust in Jesus to provide for my every need. God wants me to put him in first place in my life and make him my top priority. Then walking only in the light I start off.

Although I have no map to follow I know where I am heading. I have my ticket for the journey which no-one can take away from me. I like this analogy. My ticket has my destination on it – Heaven. I did not pay for it myself but it was paid for by Jesus and given to me as a free gift from God. Along my journey I may have lots of doubts about the way I am travelling and some people may try to convince me I am actually on the wrong road and even going in the wrong direction. At those times I can get out my ticket and reassure myself that with God as my guide and judge I cannot be on the wrong road. I would think this ticket had my photo on it, so that no-one else could use it; it is a special gift specific for my use only. The analogy falls down eventually of course. My heavenly ticket cannot be lost like an earthly one. It may get a bit deeply hidden in my pocket at times and I forget about it myself when the troubles of life crowd in. Then the Holy Spirit reminds me of my purpose and helps me to focus on where I'm heading.

Christianity can be confusing and there are so many people who insist that they are the only ones who really understand God and their way is the only true way. If you are not one of them then you are beyond the pale.

When I was first starting off I found it quite difficult to stand up, much less walk. I needed to have a strong sense of my qualifications in Christ and his acceptance of me. The bible is a wonderful book used by God as a tool to understand him and his purposes as shown throughout history and also into the future. People down the ages have held it in great esteem and suffered imprisonment and death for possessing it. I wanted to make some sense out of it also but to me it was like reading double Dutch. I knew that I needed to read it but it was dry as old bones. After many attempts I had to admit to myself that I must be doing something wrong. I was, of course, because I was trying to understand it with my own intellect alone, and I hadn't involved God in the process at all. I prayed to him to help me with this and then something wonderful happened. The passage I was reading just came alive and I had a revelation about what it meant to me. Ever since then, I can confirm to you that God's word is "… active and alive and sharper than any two-edged sword". When you study the bible with the author at your side there is certainly more than one level of understanding. As I have gone on with the Holy Spirit's guidance I find that he gives me discernment about what the passage I am reading relates to. So far I have found it may relate to

something in my life

something I need to deal with

something to pray for an individual

something to pray for in the world at large

something for general knowledge

something that will be used by him to encourage me or someone else in the future

one of God's promises

a universal truth

I started to keep a note of the Scriptures as I was led to them and the notes are very useful as a reference when I need them.

Actually, life for me was already good but I had a feeling there was something missing. I describe it like this. You can liken life to orange squash, the sort you dilute with water, and you can call it 'life'; it's good, refreshing, tasty etc. Then along comes someone who says, 'Would you like some life?' However, they give you some freshly squeezed pure orange juice. They are both called orange drink but hey, what a difference. This is really life! That was how it was for me. Outwardly everything was the same but had suddenly come alive in a new way. I saw more clearly, heard more clearly and I had become generally much more aware of everything. The birds sang so well, the flowers were especially beautiful and there seemed to be an order and design to things. I was so excited that God had placed me in this world, that he loved me and had a purpose for my life. There was hope, not just for me but for creation as a whole. God did want to communicate with me and teach and guide me and I could be part of my own destiny and his work in the world. From then on I have been practising learning to listen for God's voice, so that I can be obedient to his calling on my life and be a useful representative in the world. God is spirit and so uses his Holy Spirit to talk to my spirit. It sounds a bit "spooky", but it isn't. He won't force himself on us and we can block the Spirit's guidance at anytime, which we often do. He is not untrustworthy; he is not going to take advantage of us. There is no need for us to be suspicious of his motives, because all he wants for us is the best. We may not like what he has to say but it will certainly not be because God has it in for us or is punishing us for something.

There are so many ways in which God can communicate with us. Sometimes you can hear him speak words into your "inner ear" or he will pop a picture into your imagination. Sometimes you get an uneasy feeling about something. Often, if you've just told a lie or been deceitful, the words will come back at you and you'll be reminded of them until you've said sorry about them. Other times you will get a real excitement about a project or there is something that you know you have to get involved with. He can use other people to teach us. He uses creation to teach us. It has been said that we must listen for that "still, small voice". If we are listening, then we will hear.

God teaches me through the Holy Spirit, not just into my brain and understanding but into my spirit and heart, touching attitudes and mindsets and turning them around to be in line with his ways of light and love. As I grow in understanding he starts to bring wholeness to my life.

I wrote the following paragraphs a while ago because I felt it was important to keep a record of how God had helped me. I called it "An Amazing Maze".

Just to set the scene, I was feeling as if I was stuck in this maze. The hedges were high and thick; I couldn't see through them and I couldn't get over them or around them.

My life seemed to be going from one green impenetrable barrier to another and I was getting more tired and stressed at each turning.

I have had several phases in my life when I've felt like this. One phase I found difficult was when the children were very small. I was desperately trying to be super mum, super wife, super Christian and then make interesting and intelligent conversation as well!!

When I had small children I found it impossible to find time for a "quiet time with the Lord". Each morning you are up out of bed (usually before you've woken up) and it's full steam ahead until bedtime. Toddlers, especially, need constant attention and cannot be expected to play on their own while you do your bible study! They seem to have a knack of knowing when they haven't got your full attention. Even when an opportunity arises and you settle down for some prayer – guess what – you're straight to sleep or you can't quieten down because you're thinking of all the other things you should be doing.

At that time I had some guilt feelings about being out of touch with God and not performing the expected Christian activities. I was also very worried about bringing up the children in the right way. Should they be watching certain programmes on the telly or reading stories about magic cats and witches?

As I was struggling with all this one day, a picture popped into my mind's eye. I was this small person running about in the maze, getting nowhere fast, jumping up to try and see over the hedges. I could identify with that. Then suddenly I had a view of the maze as seen from above. I felt that God was saying to me, 'This is how I view your life – there is a pattern and design to it and it is perfect because I have made it.' For me to find that order in my life, I shall need to change my perspective. When I focus on the circumstances in my life they sometimes seem like that green hedge, looming large, a real hindrance to moving on. However, when I focus on Jesus and try to hear his voice, then I can overcome and find the way forward. I need to stop looking at the hedges and look at Jesus.

Since then, whenever I have found myself letting circumstances get the better of me, God has reminded me of that picture and the lessons learnt from it. I marvel at God because of his care and love for me. He patiently taught me in a way that I could easily understand and easily be reminded of by the Holy Spirit.

Another thing I found interesting about that picture was that God hadn't just got rid of the hedges. That obviously wasn't the problem. The problem was in how I was looking at things. I needed to learn to trust God in all things, even when in my view all was insurmountable. God says, 'As the heavens are higher than the earth, so are my ways higher than your ways and my thoughts higher than your thoughts.' *Isaiah 55: 9.*

The lessons learnt through that small picture have been the start of a training programme by God in listening to him and learning from him. I have tried to see and hear God in all I do and everywhere I go. With the help of the interpretation of the Holy Spirit I can find wisdom and strength and comfort.

Another lesson from this picture is that God is willing to intervene unconditionally in my life. It doesn't come from any worthiness on my part. I don't have to win God round with fancy prayers or magic formulas. I don't have to jump through hoops or press special buttons. This picture was a simple act of love from my Father. That really set me up for freedom. I have continued in this way with God ever since and have received such wonderful insights. I have tried to be a seeker of God in all things – sometimes the things I need are on the top as it were, for example a good sermon or seminar, a bible study or time of refreshment, but sometimes I have had to keep digging for the treasure in what can seem like a scrapheap or a desert.

So to conclude with what I have learnt from this small picture:

God is very interested in me. I see myself as Mrs Ordinary, no one special, but he sees me "Like a lily among thorns is my darling among the maidens", *Song of Songs 2:2.* He is not just interested in the "poor and needy" or the big names or someone with a story to tell but he loves me too. He obviously cares about the state I get myself into. He has taken the time to counsel me.

God can speak to me at any time and anywhere. This seems obvious but how often do I not hear because I'm not expecting to hear. Over the years, through practice, I have learnt to be aware of God's "still small voice" in lots of situations.

There is a divine plan for my life – which even has the blind alleys incorporated into it. I worry about doing the right thing and finding "God's will" for any situation. If I keep my eyes on Jesus and not my circumstances, I can then trust that I am where I am meant to be. Perhaps the blind alleys have a good purpose – and maybe it's me that is blind!

Things aren't always as we see them. God's perspective on a situation will be the true view. If I take time to enquire of the Lord he may give me some wisdom or insight to help. Even if he doesn't, I can have confidence and comfort because …

… God is in charge and can be trusted.

So to continue:

Everyone on earth can have a personal connection with God which is unique to them. We are all his children and we can call him Father. God loves us unconditionally and so we don't have to appease him constantly or be forever trying to gain his favour with sacrifices and offerings as so many others do. I know we find it hard to move away from the mindset that says achievement means worth means reward, on which our society is increasingly based. God doesn't say that at all. God wants us to love him for himself and of our own free-will, not like some robot which has no choice, or a laboratory rat being trained to certain behaviour with rewards of sweets.

The only condition to moving in his love is by accepting Jesus as the way. If we don't accept Jesus, which is our choice of course, God will still love us, but as we have chosen not to go his way he will not force us and we must be left to ourselves. This may seem okay on the surface but the implications are an eternity cut off from God. God is eternal and our spirits are eternal. So we are choosing an eternity with love or an eternity without love.

One of the first consequences of my new life was that I noticed that my irrational fears had gone. In my old life I was governed by fear. Anything vaguely dangerous was uncomfortable. I had great fears for my children and would lie awake at night imagining all sorts of dreadful scenarios involving fire or drowning!! Way before I went on holiday I would work myself up into a right state. Anyway, about a year after my conversion I realised that these fears had all gone and I hadn't noticed. I had put my trust in the maker of the universe and he could be trusted with my life and the lives of my loved ones.

Another of my friends, Jo, tells of how shortly after his journey started he was called to put his complete trust in God:

How God has worked in my life.

Twelve years ago I became a Christian, and part of that process was where I placed my life in God's hands. I moved house from Somerset to Bedford; God had already given me a job following my redundancy from a previous employer and some years later I had to move house since my role at work had changed from sales to running the factory in Hitchin.

We had tried to move house several times in the late eighties and early nineties, but the house market in Somerset was dire, and things seemed to be getting worse. The local situation was one that seemed to be going from one crisis to another; the local industry was based on farming, paper printing and the Ministry of Defence in nearby Bath. The Royal Navy had their main office in Bath, and several times the Government had said they were moving the London offices in Whitehall down to the West Country. However each time it seemed that the West Country would benefit, the door closed again. This was running concurrently with the Foot and Mouth and the BSE (Mad Cow) epidemics. Robert Maxwell had been a prominent local employer in the town, but he and his sons had raided the pension funds, and local people were desperate. Against this background of depressing news I knew that house prices were likely to start rising in the Bedford and Hitchin areas due to the steady recovery from the latest recession. The South Eastern areas near to London always showed sharp recovery when the economy started to kick away, and in late 1995 this was no exception.

I started to worry at first, but I had recently committed my life to the Lord in September by getting baptised in our local church in Midsomer Norton, and had started to believe that when God said He had great things in store for me, I had better believe Him. Well, my wife Janice and I committed to the move; our eldest son had just started senior school and the three younger children were all at school, but in a position to move without too much disruption. We prayed about it and made it known to our close friends that we needed to make the move away from the village that had been our home for the last nine years. They were extremely supportive, and prayed with us, saying they too felt that God had given me the job and therefore He would give us a suitable house. Such things were trivial to Him. As the All Powerful One and Creator of the World, we should be able to entrust one simple thing like that to Him.

We put the house on the market again, for the third time in six years, with a great deal of confidence, in February 1996. By April nothing much had happened and no-one had been to look at the house. We changed the estate agent since the first one had shown little effort in selling it; the second was more industrious and soon we had several viewings arranged. However the price still seemed to be an issue, despite various assurances from the estate agent that it was fairly well priced. We dropped the price by ten per cent and hoped that would do the trick. Nothing much seemed to be moving, and quite frankly I was starting to doubt the Almighty's abilities. I was travelling away every week on the Sunday night and staying in a B & B in Henlow where some good friends, who were also Christians, were running their small business. I was the answer to their prayers as they had been seeking to find someone to rent the room for several weeks. On the Friday I would drive the 150 miles back home and try to ask cheerfully when I got through the door how things were going. I knew exactly the situation but it seemed as if there might have been some change during my journey home.

We had decided that it was pointless looking for houses until we had sold our house as it would just lead to frustration for us if we saw something we liked before we had sold. I was becoming increasingly agitated, since being up in Hitchin I knew well that the prices were starting to move quite quickly and the choice was getting worse as all the decent properties were being snatched up. We carried on with confidence that His timing was always perfect, and with friends in both the West Country and Henlow praying for us. During the week I had started going to various events organised by the Church of some friends of mine near Bedford. They had been friends since I was at University and had become Christians several years before me. They too encouraged me to stay with the Test we had set the good Lord, and also prayed with me to ask the Lord to complete His good work.

In His inimitable way, the Lord does things when people have long since given up! I had started to have serious private doubts, but couldn't share them too openly with my friends as they kept telling me that it would happen. It was now June, and the house had been on the market for about 20 weeks. A nice family came to look at the house, put in a bid for the full price and promised to move quickly as their relocation was work related and they had no house to sell in the chain. Well, given those circumstances, you know at that point God is starting to move! At last we could start to look for a house.

We had been looking in general terms at the areas we liked and the places we could afford, given the price differential between the South West and the Home Counties. Within a few days our friends in Bedford had found a house in the very same area where they lived. We knew the schools were excellent and had an outstanding reputation since the league tables and house prices tended to reflect these points. Funnily enough, we spent ages trying to find alternative houses to the one our friends had found. I say funnily enough because when we went to see the house they thought was just perfect, we didn't think too much to it.

They had prayed about it and heard God say very clearly that it was our house, but I think we were deaf to that prayer at that time. It is strange how we test Him sometimes, as well as He tests us. I had started to believe that He was really behind these events when almost every other house we were interested in was either sold before we could look at it or we separately or together decided that the houses were not for us.

The main reason that neither of us thought too much to the house was that it needed so much work; quite frankly it was a wreck. The roof leaked, the guttering was all blocked and no-one had lived in it for several months. The main attractions, however, were the location and the price. The lady who owned it had been the victim of her husband's gambling problems, and had to sell the house. She had met someone else and just wanted to get out of the mess she was in, and everyone who had looked at it had gone away in despair or found a better property. We went back several times to look at it, each time with severe reservations about the amount of work needed. Each time our friends had told us the house was ours, and that they knew it to be right for us. It was a large four bedroomed house, and had a nice sized garden just right for bringing up the growing family. It was in the best village from the children's point of view, with a superb primary and middle school right in the village.

We talked together and prayed. Then for the first time we talked to the lady who was selling the house; on every other occasion we had been seen by the estate agent. She was such a nice lady, very trusting, and instantly took a liking to our children and us. She let us have the keys to come in and look round the place, even when she was not around, bearing in mind she now lived several miles away, and the place was deserted. She shared some of her circumstances and explained fully and frankly how the house had come to be sold. Her honesty shone out and we took her at face value, knowing that she had told us everything about the house when she could have kept much of it hidden. We decided at last to give in and accept God's present. We put in the offer the very next day; it was accepted, of course.

It was now the middle of August and the chances of meeting the deadline of moving out of the house we had sold to meet the buyer's requirement was now looking difficult but extremely tight. Our solicitor had done everything he could to move all the pieces of paper as fast as possible. We had heard that people could exchange contracts within three to four weeks, but never met anyone who had succeeded in this feat. We were going to give it a good try at least, with the new school term looming and the possibility of sharing our friends in Bedford's house for a few days as a fall back situation.

The "small miracles" now came thick and fast. Our solicitor had never had a return back from the local authority so fast. It turned out later that the lady who does these forms went to our church. She didn't know us at all at that time, but just felt the Lord say that she needed to get this particular form back. We found out later on that year that she had processed the form, since her husband ended up working on the house as the builder who did the repairs. The Land Registry forms all arrived safely and everything was in order. The solicitor started to believe we could meet the deadline, and although he was very professional in his approach, kept pushing the other solicitors to keep up their work.

All seemed well until disaster struck two days before the final exchange of contracts. Our solicitor found an outstanding debt from a court giving one of the big banks power to hold part ownership of the property. In other words, the property would not belong totally to the lady selling it until a grant relinquishing the debt had been given by the bank. This posed considerable problems for our solicitor, and should have been found and cleared weeks before by the solicitors for the lady selling the property. It seemed as if this one event could stop the whole process dead in its tracks. Our solicitor advised us of this on the evening of the day we had packed up the entire house into the removals' van and said goodbye to the whole village. It seemed the ultimate challenge for us – did we really believe God had "done His good works" for us or not?

After a cup of tea and a "chat" with our solicitor at 5pm, Janice and I decided we had to carry on despite his professional advice that we could lose the whole house on this one event. I asked him if he would have done the same thing in my place. He said he wouldn't, but off the record there was a small chance that it would all work out provided the documents could be cleared. However we knew that we were leaving the village to follow the removals' van to a place that could not be ours for several days. The one "saving grace" was that the lady selling the house had already given me the keys to her house; such was her trust in us. The solicitor agreed it was extremely unlikely they would "evict" us after we had moved our belongings into the house. It was extremely unusual, but he would try to complete the exchange after we had moved into the house. Obviously he knew we had the keys to the house, but the other solicitors did not. Janice and I had a sense of calm about the whole event that surprised even our closest friends, even though they had prayed for us.

We followed the van the 150 miles I had driven so often in the last year. It was to park up overnight and then meet us the following day in Oakley, a village near Bedford, our new home. Meanwhile we were to stay with our friends in the same village. All six of us mixed in with their family made eleven in the house. We arrived close to midnight, having had an extremely long day; it was quite an emotional occasion. We regaled them with the details and they felt the same sense of calm I had felt when we made the decision to leave the village earlier that day. It was all in the hands of someone so much more powerful than me.

We moved into the house on the Wednesday. The lady who had sold the house visited us on the day just to make sure we were fine. She was so supportive of the whole event, and was extremely happy that we were going to make the place of which she had unhappy memories a happy place with our family. The contracts were finally exchanged on the Friday, much to everyone in the legal profession's relief. They had found the bank and obtained the release papers, again in record time. The house was finally ours.

Strangely enough, both Janice and I inherited enough money from relatives over the next 12 months totally to repair and rebuild the house. God hadn't forgotten our every need, and provided the means to complete His Perfect work in us. All we had to do was keep believing in Him to provide for our needs. We still live there happily today in a place that is worth far more than we could have afforded, given our difficult circumstances in moving from a lower to a higher priced area. We still enjoy His blessings today and thank Him for His Grace and Goodness.

Chapter Three

A Sense of Direction

As I travel on with God I will try to learn to hear his voice. I will only be travelling in the light and will need to rest. How many of us can do that easily? I know I find it difficult to allow myself time off.

God's ways of doing things are so different to the ways of the world. In the bible it says that the two are actually opposed to each other. When we need to rest from work in the world we often indulge in some sort of leisure activity. Jesus said to his disciples, however, when they were weary, 'Come away with me and rest.' My refreshment along my journey will be by taking time out to be alone with Jesus, in quality time of prayer, praise and listening, for as long as it takes and not just when I can fit it into my busy schedule. As I submit myself to him he takes away my weariness and refreshes me with his Holy Spirit and I am ready to continue in whatever he has called me to do.

I think doing this regularly will help to keep us in the right attitude as to whom we are and how we match up to the very great might and majesty of God Almighty. He has told us not to think too highly of ourselves and by coming into a sense of his presence we will keep ourselves from becoming proud and unusable. I also think we need to be honest with God. I know this sounds obvious but we often try to hide our true motives from God and even from ourselves. When my children were small and they wanted something, sometimes they would try and be good to win my favour before they asked me for it and we are like that with God sometimes as well. For example I may catch myself thinking along these sorts of lines – 'I'd better get God in a good mood with me first by thanking and praising and then I will ask him' or 'I'd better not seem greedy and I'll put other people's requests first before I ask for myself'. Whereas to God we are so transparent and he sees right into our hearts and knows what we want before we've even formed the request into words. I don't like it when my children try and manipulate me and so it must be so much worse for God when I do the same to him. When I come to God with a burden on my heart for whatever reason – I may be angry with someone, hurt, weighed down with doubts and confusion, grieving, rejected, excited about something, in wonder about something discovered – whatever it is, I get it off my chest first. God is big enough to handle it because He is not like us. As we offload onto him he can heal us. As we empty our hearts He will fill them, but the emptying must come first.

The Psalms are a very good example of this. In many of them the writer is absolutely livid about something but by the end of the Psalm, after ranting and raving before God and asking for all sorts of curses to fall on his enemies, he has had a change of heart and God has worked a little miracle on him. By coming into the sanctuary of God's presence we can start to understand the magnitude of his love and purposes. By excluding ourselves deliberately from God's presence on false premises we miss the healing and blessings God promises us. The Psalms are so human and relevant even today, but ultimately give us an exuberant insight into the character of God.

God wants us to approach him as a child to its father, with confidence, not childish but childlike, with openness, honesty and trust. Many people don't have a good relationship with their earthly father and so don't have a good role model for a relationship with the Heavenly Father. However, I'm sure we can all respond to how we feel a Heavenly Father should be. He is the best Father imaginable. He is always there for us and not just for the important events in our life. He is on our side and wants the best for us. He loves us more than anyone ever could and doesn't turn it on and off. He is absolutely trustworthy and his promises last forever. He loves us so much that he is willing to discipline us and not let us get away with excusing ourselves for our bad behaviour. He listens to us and wants to have a meaningful relationship with us.

This next example shows how God taught me to heed his voice in my everyday life and take him seriously wherever I am and whatever I am doing.

I had loaded the shopping into the car at the supermarket and was ready to drive home when I was aware of a voice in my head, which I understood to be the Lord, saying, 'You are going to have an accident.'

I really didn't know what to do. I reviewed the options in my mind. Perhaps I had imagined it but then again it had come out of the blue and so I had to believe it was from God and therefore for my good. Maybe I should leave the car in the car park and get a taxi home – but then I might have an accident involving the taxi. Whatever I did about getting home involved opportunity for accidents!! The strange thing was there was no element of fear and I didn't panic.

In the end I just took some time to pray in the car along these sorts of lines. Thank you God for letting me know this will happen, help me to be alert as I drive home and please let there be no harm done.

I was extremely careful driving home but as I turned into my road I bumped into the back of a car which had stopped to turn right. No-one was injured and there was minor damage to the cars.

I know other people would perhaps put a different slant to this incident but it made me aware of God's voice in my life. His word is true and you'd better believe it. The accident happened as he said it would. He hadn't said, 'You will have an accident if …' There was no if.

The following illustrations from two of my friends show how God can guide us when we are prepared to listen. Firstly, Patsy gives an account of how God's guidance has had a lasting effect on the course of her life.

How I became involved in the Painting Retreats

This particular morning I was feeling lonely and downhearted: it seemed that however hard I had tried, life was really difficult. It was a Thursday morning in September, the boys had gone off to school and I was just clearing up the breakfast things when the door bell rang. On opening the door I was greeted by a neighbour, Muriel Shells, who lived at the Cloisters next door, and an unknown gentleman who turned out to be Muriel's brother, Canon Charles Shells.

He explained that he'd been given my name by two people in connection with art teaching and asked if he could come in and have a cup of coffee with me and tell me about the Painting and Prayer retreats he ran and how I possibly could help him!

So Muriel left to go shopping and Canon Shells came in and told me how he'd started these Painting Retreats and that he was needing one or two more tutors and he'd very much like me to be one. He was in the process of compiling his prospectus for the following year and offered me a date for the coming June. I was overwhelmed at the speed of all this and felt completely inadequate to take on this responsibility – it would mean working as an art tutor, with him as Chaplain, for a week, in a situation completely new to me – as well as the fact that it was many months hence and I was responsible for the boys and didn't know what might be happening by then. Anyway, he said he'd give me some time to think about it, and when I asked him when he'd like my answer he said he'd give me till after breakfast the next day!

My head was in a flat spin and I prayed very hard about the situation. However hard I tried to say 'no' to Canon Shells' request I found I couldn't – even though I still felt inadequate. In my thinking I was aware that this "situation" had <u>come</u> to me and was not of my own volition – so, trusting that God's hand was in this I decided that if He wanted me to do this He would give me whatever was needed to accomplish it satisfactorily (and the boys would be watched over).

So, I agreed to be the art tutor the following June at the Llangasty Retreat House in a lovely part of Wales near Brecon Beacons, which Charles described as his heaven on earth!

When it came to a week before the Retreat I had absolutely no idea how I was going to get to that remote part of Wales by public transport: I knew I could get as far as Bath and then – a blank. Again I prayed and trusted that God would guide me and open up the way, and two days before I was due to travel the phone went and Charles Shells said he'd be in Hitchin and would I like to travel to

Llangasty in his car with him? That was such a blessing and relief to me for which I really thanked God.

The whole Retreat was very special (and significant to me as it was Pentecost), the surroundings were glorious, the weather fine and I met some lovely people. It was as if one particular lady, who'd been on these retreats quite a few times previously, was "allocated" by God to help me. She just quietly and sensitively told me what was expected of me at different times – reassessment of work, setting up the exhibition etc. There was also someone else there who was supportive and prayed with me when I felt unsure of myself. The whole group of between 15 and 20 people gelled together so quickly and we were a very happy family. Some were missionaries on sabbatical who'd come for refreshment; many had come away from great trauma, including the lovely warm-hearted priest from South Africa who spoke to us of the terrible Apartheid troubles. It was such a privilege to be with them all. Everyone, however "ordinary" they might seem on the outside, had a story to tell and was special – which we all are in God's eyes. The week was demanding but really rewarding and I came back refreshed and energised and God has encouraged me to extend myself and develop my skills.

As for my homeward journey, my new friend offered me a lift as far as Bath and I caught the London train from there. I settled comfortably in my seat and was thinking that at last I'd be able to read the book I'd brought with me and really get into it, as it was a fairly long journey ahead – but I hadn't read more than about two paragraphs when the lady sitting opposite me said, 'Excuse me, but that looks a very interesting book you're reading; could you tell me about it?' As I'd only just started the book I wasn't able to explain much (the book was "Healing the Family Tree" by Dr Kenneth McAll) and the title really intrigued her. As it was about Christian healing it opened up a chance for her to talk and she plied me with questions on aspects of Christianity all the way to Paddington! I told her of different books I'd read and touched on their witness and she wanted to know where to find these books. She was just hungry for information and all I had to do was to give simple and straightforward answers.

After we'd said goodbye at Paddington (with her keen to find out more) a young mother with a little boy in her arms came up to me and said, 'I don't suppose you noticed us in the carriage but I couldn't help hearing what you were saying, and it was just so good to hear Christ glorified.' I'd been completely unaware that others might be listening, or of how God had been working until this lady spoke to me. It is amazing how, even if you've never met someone before and you're both Christians, you can feel so bonded together. This is how I felt that Saturday afternoon at Paddington with this young mother and her little boy and they waved me off on my next train with such warmth and affection.

When I arrived at Kings Cross my third train was just ready to leave and on arriving in Hitchin I straightaway bumped into a friend who said, 'You look loaded Patsy, would you like a lift home?' (This was the first time in all the years I'd lived in Hitchin that that had ever happened to me – so I piled into her car with my suitcase and painting equipment and books and was driven to my door!)

I really felt that God was telling me in all sorts of ways that He wanted me to do these Painting Retreats and that he could supply my needs by showing how he could get me from door to door (with some interesting little detours on the way) and I'm still involved with them twenty years later, going to more special places and meeting more special people.

My friend Jo would like to share with us an incident in her life where God has intervened in a powerful way.

One of God's Surprises

It was one of those moments when you say to yourself, 'It's no good – I have to do something about it.' So I booked an appointment with my doctor – (I must confess I didn't pray about it). But my knee had become so painful I often fell over sideways if I knelt down.

My doctor examined my knee and announced that I had a common problem known to the medical profession as "sago grains"! He added there was no cure and I would have to learn to live with it – that is, with the help of a small tube of cream which he would prescribe – some to be rubbed on twice daily.

I returned home and repeated the diagnosis to John. 'Well, there you are then – you'll have to do as the doctor says and put up with it.'

'No I won't,' I replied. 'God doesn't want me to have a painful knee for the rest of my life. He's a God who heals.'

By the next morning I had put it out of my mind and busied myself around the house. I was on my knees washing the bathroom floor when I realised my knee was no longer painful. I moved it this way and that – crawled around – carefully put some weight on it – stood up and walked up and down – then I jumped for joy and shouted 'Hallelujah' – my knee was healed and it has been fine ever since.

My husband Geoff gives an example of how he felt supported at an important point in his life when he needed to put his trust in God and not rely on his own resources:

My first memorable encounter with "He who made the world and everything in it" was in 1983. At that time I was working for Post Office Telephones (which became BT in 1984) as a Technical Officer based at Hitchin Telephone Exchange. I had been promoted to that grade ten years earlier and was looking for further advancement into "management". A local promotion to the next grade (Assistant Executive Engineer – AEE for short) was virtually unknown at that time and those keen to get on had to apply for a promotion board in London. This I did and was fortunate to be given a date for a promotion board. This was something completely outside my experience as one who was used to driving a big yellow van with a cartoon of Busby on the side, not mixing with senior managers at BT Headquarters. I duly prepared myself for the big day and, dressed in my best (only) suit, caught the train to Kings Cross. Once on the train, however, I became so panic-stricken, convincing myself that I could not go through with this, that I almost got off the train at the next stop in order to head for home. Then I remembered what I had heard preached about so many times; that we are not alone, that God is always with us wherever we go and whatever we do. I started to pray and by the time I arrived at Kings Cross a tremendous sense of peace, an at-oneness with God, came over me and I knew that whatever the outcome of the interview it was God's will and had been part of his plan for me since time began. As it turned out, I failed the interview on that occasion but was successful at a similar interview 12 months later.

I am reminded of an incident several years ago when I was working part-time at a local playgroup while my children were still quite young. This particular day there were two things I wanted to do between finishing work and picking the children up from school at ten past three. One was to do the shopping and the other was to visit my step-grandfather, whom I called Uncle Tom, in his nursing home as he was quite poorly. I hadn't yet worked out how I was going to fit in doing both.

Anyway when I got to work my friend Barbara, who runs the playgroup, reminded me that we were both booked in for a training session straight after playgroup had finished for the morning, which was being held in the council offices in town, and asked if I'd remembered my packed lunch. I hadn't and had actually forgotten all about the training session. Well at least that had made any decisions about what to do after work easy – I'd be doing neither option.

After playgroup had finished Barbara and I went off in her car to the training session, planning to stop off at Sainsbury's to get me a sandwich. We were nearly out of the car park when she realised we hadn't locked up properly or something like that, I can't remember the exact details. So we went back and put that right and then started off again. Barbara managed to scrape the car on the post at the exit to the car park. There was no real damage done to the car or the post but by now time was getting on and we were starting to get a bit stressed! We reached Sainsbury's and I got out to buy a sandwich while Barbara parked the car. I was in the queue and realised I'd no money for the sandwich. I had to put it back and return to the car to find Barbara. I'd had enough by then and after talking it over with Barbara we decided to go back to her house for lunch and book into another training session another time.

Over lunch we reviewed the morning's events and wondered if perhaps God was trying to get through to us. After consideration we decided that I could probably rustle up a meal with the ingredients I had at home and the shopping could wait until tomorrow. My first priority should be to drive over to see Uncle Tom, which was what I did. He was very poorly but I had an opportunity to spend some time with him and have a chat. He died during that night and I was so glad that we had heeded the promptings from God – eventually!

Chapter Four

When Difficulties Arise

To become a Christian doesn't mean that God is going to take all our troubles away, wave his magic wand and make everything better. He could do it but that isn't necessarily what would be the best for us in the long run. We are in the world and the rain has to fall on the good and the bad at the same time. Jesus tells us that we are to expect all sorts of troubles in life but that when we involve God in the situation, the circumstances may not change but with his help we can overcome and cope with the situation.

One immediate response to an unpleasant or difficult situation is 'why me' or 'what have I done to deserve this'. The spirit, however, teaches us that our self-preservation should not be our overwhelming priority. Our life is not our own any more. We are God's servants and have been bought at a very high price. We must each be willing to lay down our life, as he did, if he asks us to. He says that anything we put ahead of him (in the place that rightly should be his) will be as if we are worshipping an idol. This applies even if that something is a good thing in its own right. God wants us to be wholly available to him. I'm not saying that we should treat our life as worthless because it is a wonderful gift from God and should be respected, as also should the lives of others, but when our own life is more important to us than anything else, then the balance is wrong.

The strange thing about all this is that as we relinquish to him more ownership of things and loves in our life, He will actually receive them from us – and then he may give them back doubled or trebled. People have witnessed to the fact that as they let go of trying to control their family and work things out for the best as they see it, God has mended family relationships and given them more love for each other.

Sometimes I think we are our own worst enemies; we get in God's way and try to tell him what is best. We like to be the chairman and set the agenda but we need to stand aside and let God take the role of leadership in our life. It's easy to have all the words but I know that sometimes when the going gets tough, it's hard even to pray. Even when you haven't the strength to know anything or even form the words, 'help, help', so long as you can imagine yourself turning to face him, he will understand and meet you in your need.

My friend Celia has had many problems in her life. She has MS and her marriage has broken down. She has written a poem about one aspect of her life:

Housebound

There is a place,

An actuality

With plants and trees

And air that moves.

Sun that shines, maybe,

Space around things

And smiles to greet the folk who

Be outside.

You watch from gilded cage

Those people in real life,

Your life a narrow road

From stage to stage.

The care you get provides

Essential elements,

Your basic needs are met

With transient glancing aid.

A joke, a smile inside a parcelled job,

They give their time and then move on

And to another case

The same but different sadness.

Inside alone once more

The clock keeps running on.

What next, what progress is in sight?

Seize it with verve – it will not wait.

A friend, a precious friend calls in

With love to share, to ease the discontent.

What can be done when life is cruel,

That love is priceless, time is too.

God sees it all. He will not leave.

Trust that he leads – it will be well

Not what I planned

He'll see the route – a mystery to me.

Born to decline – no, that's not me.

I have the spirit inside to flourish and grow

I will win as much as can be

No limit to my will – I can consider all

With God on my side – the light will shine

The shadows may threaten at times –

I'll not wither or pine

There is a mountain to be scaled.

It's arduous but what a view!

It's worth all the toil

Just to pull through

Though sadness will pour on scorn.

A life of such beauty, love and openness, I'll see

Ne'er-do-wells defeated – what a score

To prosper and live as full as can be

Giving and taking – a fair trade to make.

Joy in the morning after tears in the night

God will abate anger

And demonstrate might

Just hang on in there and wait for His time.

Ps 30: 5. For his anger endureth but a moment; in his favour is life: weeping may endure for a night, but joy cometh in the morning.

Another friend, Joan, writes about the strength she receives from God on a daily basis and especially at a time in her life when her daughter was very ill.

What is a Christian?

This is something I have asked myself so many times and my answer is in my heart and with me from the moment I wake each morning until I sleep at the end of the day. I ask the Lord for his guidance and pray that what I am doing is his will. I am sure each follower of Jesus has his own interpretation of what a "good" Christian is and how a "good" Christian should practise his faith but how to carry out this deed is a task in itself and from the moment I became at one with the Lord, life seemed to take on a new dimension. I had always imagined that following the way of Jesus in true belief would make life so much easier in a way of definitely knowing what was right and what was wrong. In reality, it can be like driving down the motorway the wrong way, with all the other traffic coming straight towards you. Aiming to carry out a Christian way of life is the most magnificent, beautiful and challenging experience and in no way does it make life easier but it does make it more fulfilling. There are many of us who continue our everyday lives trying to do our best in God's way; perhaps turning to the Bible and relying on our prayer to speak to God for confirmation that what we are doing is his will.

We so often hear of revelations when criminals, outcasts or addicts come to the calling of Christ and find their lives turned around because they have found Christianity. For the rest of us who turn our lives to God, the call will occur in the same astounding clarity but experiences may vary. Some know the difference immediately; for others it is more gradual. When we receive Christ, we become children of

God. Those who become Christians become new people. They are not the same any more, for the old is gone. A new life has begun! To God though, we are each important just as we are, all his chosen children and each of us of equal importance. Isn't that a miracle in itself? One of the prophets of the Bible, Isaiah, tells us that God says, 'I have called you by name and you are my own. When you pass through deep waters, I am with you …'

My own personal experiences with God are very real, particularly when our daughter was unwell. We have been very lucky and she is now healthy. There were many times when God seemed very far away but numerous friends and also people we did not even know were praying for us. This gave me so much strength and without this comfort and support I could not have carried the overwhelming feeling of anguish, knowing how much we had to make someone so young endure, in the way of pain and being so ill and distressed. Since that time, I have experienced an almost alien awareness of "privilege" to have been in that predicament and sometimes I feel God wanted me to experience that situation in order to bring me closer to him. He knew He was the lifeline and it would teach me to pray and believe in Him. We do not always fully comprehend His way of working and sometimes it is very difficult to put our complete trust in Him, especially at a testing time.

Perhaps when we see illness and suffering in the world and feel upset, we should realise that it is a mere glimpse at the agonising torture God has to endure. He really wants to help and have us turn to Him as we are his children and the enormity of what He has to endure is beyond our comprehension. THANK YOU GOD – I LOVE YOU.

I would like to include here another incident from my husband, Geoff:

My second encounter was early in the morning the day after my father died in August 1996. He had had to have his leg amputated (at age 87) about 20 months before and had since spent his time in and out of hospital and at Foxholes Nursing Home. He had just celebrated his 58th wedding anniversary and his 89th birthday when he was taken back into hospital with an infection. We were on holiday at the time and got back in time to visit him at the Lister – he died early in the afternoon the day after. I awoke early the following morning and was completely enveloped in a warm glow and felt utterly at peace. I felt my dad's presence (my perception was that he was a young man again) with the message that he was free of pain, he was happy to be where he was, everything was OK, he was with Jesus and that we would meet again one day. This feeling faded but returned to a lesser degree several times between his death and the day of his funeral.

This encounter reinforced my faith and belief that there is life after death, that one day we will meet loved ones who have gone before us and that we should never doubt the message of the Cross and the Resurrection of Jesus Christ, the Lord and Saviour of mankind.

These are three very different examples of real help and comfort in times of need and I find them very powerful and moving accounts. No-one gets through life without some sort of trauma at one time or another. We all need comfort and understanding and God is able to provide that for us. So if you're reading this and you are going through a difficult time and can't see any way out – try not to despair but try a prayer. Keep alert for an answer. It may come when you are not expecting it or in an unexpected way and you have nothing to lose, but everything to gain. Sometimes we already know the answer, deep down, and perhaps need to face something in our lives that needs attention before we can move on. Often I have found that just when I have needed it God has provided a friend, or someone with a hug or a friendly face, to lift my spirit and give me hope. He doesn't necessarily give us a way out of our problems but a way through them and wisdom for how to deal with them.

The next piece is from my friend Ann. She shows how God has intervened in her life, changing difficult situations into positive opportunities to show her his love and to use her in his world to help others:

I first became aware of God in my life when I was childminding. I had hoped, and indeed it had been an ambition from early childhood, to have six children of my own. I experienced many troubled times and was advised to be content with my two beautiful daughters. I was, but still had so much to share. So after a friend approached me, I set out on what was to be a fifteen year career as a childminder. Sharing my love with many children, sometimes as short term emergency foster parent, I believe God had influenced my life and it was his will that was being done.

Later on I was very aware of God's presence after my interview for my first "proper" job for many years. I had applied for a job at a local primary school. For interview I had to present myself to a panel of staff and governors and "sell" myself in five to ten minutes. I was petrified, especially when I saw the competition, looking every bit the part with folders of evidence and looking very businesslike. However, I came out of the interview room convinced that God had taken over, as it certainly wasn't me conducting myself so eloquently. I got the job.

One of my most recent encounters with God was during a bout of ill health. I had developed a deep vein thrombosis in my left leg and had subsequently had to cancel a trip to Canada. I was off school but could "potter". I think my idea differed from that of the consultant and I hurt my back, causing me great pain.

One Wednesday Jane Fox (our vicar) came to administer communion; she read a bible passage, the one where a sick woman touches Jesus' cloak. It was soon after that encounter that I recovered my strength and thank God was able to return to a normal life.

Chapter Five

Observations Along the Way

God uses his creation to teach us about himself and all sorts of things. Many of our medicines are made from plant derivatives for example. His design style shows throughout the natural world and can be seen in the same way you would recognise the style of an artist or composer. I love seeing what he has made; the great power and forces of nature are awesome. I have only recently started travelling abroad and I love flying, looking down with a "God's eye" view on all the different landscapes.

Cathy shares with us the lesson she learnt whilst on holiday:

God's Houseplant

Some years ago while on holiday, we had the opportunity to take a two-mile hike through a rainforest. We started out at daybreak, our tour guide leading us up through the forest to a 100 ft waterfall. The path was narrow, wet and often slippery. At intervals our guide would stop to point out trees and plants – their beautiful flowers, fruit and medicinal property so highly valued by the original settlers. He told us that all of the rainforest plants were the close relatives of our houseplants. He also pointed out that however well we treat our houseplants, they may reward us with flowers but will never produce fruit. Why? Houseplants don't have any urgency in life.

Over the next few days I thought about my plants. They lived a fairly comfortable life, yet they were not as strong and healthy as their rainforest cousins, who appeared to thrive in adverse conditions. The stressed environment of the rainforest enabled them to produce fruit that supported an abundance of forest life.

I began to draw a parallel between the houseplant and my own life. I liked to think of my family and myself surrounded by God's love and protection. When trials came my way, I expected God to deal with them for me. If He didn't, I felt He had somehow let me down. I began to realise that I would never grow to be an effective Christian if I always expected God to protect me from adversity. I asked the Lord's forgiveness, and asked Him to teach me how to face my own adversity so I could grow in His strength and wisdom.

Since that day many trials have come my way, but I have tried to seek the Lord's perspective and guidance in every situation. He has honoured my prayer, revealing His will and sharing His wisdom and strength with me.

Just recently, I read **James,** *Chapter One, with a commentary entitled "Happy Adversity". James encourages his readers to consider their trials as nothing but joy. I can't honestly profess to have reached a stage where I can embrace trials with joy but I do understand what James is saying. He knew that trials were a test of faith that would produce endurance and maturity. Adversity doesn't come to steal our happiness but to bring the gift of staying power, enabling us to produce spiritual fruits that strengthen our faith and support others in their trials. So I hope you will forgive me for taking this opportunity to wish you 'Happy Adversity'.*

Another incident, that could easily have been missed, is told by Martin, and shows that wherever you are you should have your ears and eyes open for that "still, small voice":

The Wonder of Creation

It was October time and coming up to Hallowe'en and there was a party being planned – not just any party but a fancy dress party – and it was decided that there needed to be at least one witch at the party. It was then that we began to put together the items that a witch would require; among them we needed a broomstick – you know the kind, a handle with lots of long twigs attached to it, so it looked like one of those brooms that you use to sweep up leaves in a garden.

Well, we didn't have such a thing, so I took my young daughter to a wood just outside Hitchin, parked the car and together we began to collect the twigs we needed. It was a sunny day and the sun shone through the trees, spilling its light and warmth into the wood. Suddenly my daughter took my hand and pointed to a tiny flower (I can't remember what it was) that was bathed in sunlight. She looked at me and said, 'Daddy, did God make that flower for me?' For what seemed like a couple of minutes, probably just a few seconds, the whole world seemed to stand still, and all too briefly we could see creation as God had made it, and it felt as if God was in the wood with us, appreciating the work he had done. There are no words to describe the way I felt, but to know that we stood in God's creation was awe-inspiring.

The beauty of the moment was broken by the sound of a deer crashing its way through the undergrowth, frightening my daughter and making her cry. In the next second everything had returned to the way it was before. It was and still is a time in my life that I will never forget. And yes, we did make the broomstick for the party that went ahead.

Sometimes I feel that I hear God more clearly when contemplating my surroundings, rather than in Church, where there is often a busy, noisy atmosphere and no space to listen.

My example is:

When I was sitting quietly in my living room one day, praying and looking out of the window, I had an interesting experience. We have a very small garden but in one corner there is an apple tree. This day the sun had just come out after a heavy downpour of rain. It was bright and I was blinded by a particularly piercing ray that was being bounced off a single raindrop on a leaf. It was so intense that it disturbed me and I had to move. It started me thinking.

My thoughts turned to light and water. The bible often uses these elements to illustrate the characteristics of God. God is light and the Holy Spirit is often referred to as being the water of life.

The sunlight shines in the world just as God's light shines in the world, illuminating the truth for all to see. The raindrops fall just as tears fall in sorrow and weeping. The grieving and tears of the world can go unnoticed, in general, as the raindrop on the leaf is barely visible, but when the light of God falls on it, then our compassion burns with an intensity that is directed and can make an impact and stir up people to action.

Alan's contribution shows just how much he trusts in God wherever he is in the world and whatever he is doing. Wherever he goes he sees the hand of God at work and he is encouraged:

I have included these thoughts as they serve to remind me that God is never very far away, wherever one is in the world.

The first time I travelled to Hong Kong in 1987 it was to present a paper at a conference. It was the first time I had travelled outside Europe. When I arrived in Hong Kong I knew no-one and felt very alone. That evening I ate alone and then walked to the conference centre. I asked to see the room where we would make our presentations the next day to familiarize myself with the surroundings. As I walked back along the waterfront I began to feel more confident about my presentation. The next morning I arrived early at the conference and was greeted by another delegate who was Polish. He welcomed me and later I found out he was a Roman Catholic. My presentation was timed for late morning and followed a distinguished American speaker who had an international reputation. My thoughts were, 'How can I follow that?' At the coffee break the American came over to me, introduced himself, and said, 'I'm a Presbyterian; I hope God has blessed you today. I'm looking forward to hearing your paper.' This short conversation certainly gave me confidence and two years later after another conference the American arranged for one of my papers to be published in the USA.

Some of my other experiences whilst travelling include:

When in Cologne, I always visit the Crypt of the Cathedral where there are reputed to be the remains of the three magi. There is a special feeling about this church; it is outstandingly tall and has a very ornate ceiling which is viewed by looking into mirrors. Cologne suffered intensive bombing during the Second World War and whilst all the surrounding area was destroyed, the Cathedral remained intact. I have visited the Cathedral at least ten times since 1972 and always light a candle whilst there.

I was woken by a brass band at 6.00am in Fosombrone (Marche, Italy) on St Cecilia's Day (Patron Saint of music). I had travelled to Italy on business, arriving late in the evening and finally getting to my hotel at about 1.30am. The arrangements were for me to have a good night's sleep and be collected at 9.30am to be driven to the company's design studio for the day. The tradition of the area is to celebrate this anniversary with a brass band performance at daybreak. On this occasion the celebration started just below my bedroom window.

After a Saturday evening fashion show in Paris we were sightseeing and visited the church at Sacré Coeur during a Sunday Service. It is apparently normal practice for tourists to process around the aisles during services. It is fascinating to see both the church and the congregation but difficult to think of this happening at Holy Saviour Church during the 9.30 Eucharist.

In the late 1990s I worked regularly in Dublin and during the drive down from the airport to the city I noticed that the taxi drivers "cross" themselves when driving past a church. This was usually around 8.30am so I am unsure if it was the time of day or the time of a service.

I have included some of the prayers and readings that have encouraged me over many years:

Prayers:

Dear Lord, open our hearts that we hear your voice; show us your will and give us the grace to follow it for ever. Amen.

Dear Lord, I pray for my family, friends and all those who have no-one to pray for them today. Bind us in your love, care and protection; keep your angels with us and give us the strength and courage so that all we do today is in your name and to your glory. Amen.

The Lord's Prayer.

Readings:

2 Timothy 3, vs. 16 – 17

No-one stood by me the first time I had to defend myself; all deserted me. May God not count it against them. But the Lord stayed with me and gave me strength, so that I was able to proclaim the full message for all the Gentiles to hear; and I was rescued from being sentenced to death.

1 Corinthians 13, vs. 4 – 7

Love is patient and kind; it is not jealous or conceited or proud; love is not ill-mannered or selfish or irritable: love does not keep a record of wrongs; love is not happy with evil, but is happy with the truth. Love never gives up; and its faith, hope and patience never fail.

Try reading the above passage and replacing the word "love" with your own name.

Chapter Six

Résumé

If you have found these illustrations interesting – of how God loves us and is prepared to join with us in the process of living out our lives – and would like to start on this journey for yourself, you must follow the way of Jesus:

Firstly, have a good look at yourself, compared to the perfect. Admit to yourself and God that there are things you should not have done, said or thought, and there are also things you should have done, that you haven't.

Say sorry to God for all those things you've identified; lay them all before him in your mind and be willing to leave them with him to deal with. Ask him to forgive you. Turn your back on them; do not take them up again but believe that God has forgiven you.

Ask Jesus to come into your life with his Holy Spirit so that you can put the past behind you. You can then move forward, with his help, and in his strength alone, into what life holds for you.

Obtain a bible and start to read it. Some of the passages below will help you understand your position as a new creation. With the Holy Spirit's guidance you will be led to revelations about Jesus for the renewing of your mind and your spiritual growth in the knowledge and love of the Lord.

My advice is to learn to listen to God for yourself. He wants us to be able to respond to him personally and immediately. We're not much use to the Lord if we have to keep running to someone else to check on the message! Bible commentaries and daily notes are interesting and can be useful but should definitely not be a substitute for a personal relationship and do not build up our own discernment of the things of God. Keep a journal of the passages you are led to each day and over the weeks you will be able to look back and see the Lord's hand in guiding you. It does take a bit of perseverance though, because it is so new.

Listen to God before you listen to man! Walking with God is not simply an intellectual or academic exercise but a living, breathing way of life. When you are in tune with God he will use what you hear and read to teach you what you need to know. Of course he uses men and women to teach and instruct, but we accept what we hear and have understanding of what is taught by the Holy Spirit working in us. We can learn interesting things from bible studies and sermons but it is only when you have been taught something through the Spirit, directly from the Lord, that it sticks with you and you grow from it. Lots of people sit under good teaching for years and never grow. If the Spirit isn't there, then there is no life to your knowledge. The things of God will keep the mind and intellect stretched for even the cleverest of individuals.

Your place in Jesus is the building block of faith, something that once truly understood is the firm foundation for life. Some people make the mistake of believing that because they do good works or are nice people this then proves that they are Christians and have been saved. It doesn't work like that. The correct flow of things is this – salvation comes only as a free gift from God; we do not deserve it or earn it. We cannot boast of, nor have faith in, our own achievements. The good works and other benefits of being a Christian only come from the faith we have in our position in Jesus. In first place should be your relationship with God, firmly based on your salvation through Jesus. This is the way it should flow, like streams of water from the spring.

Ask the Lord to lead you to a local church community and get baptised. Join with other Christians and meet with them for encouragement and worship and prayer. Support each other and reach out to the people around you. Be useful and willing to obey God's leading in your life.

Useful Bible Passages

From the New Testament

Hebrews 8: 10–13.

"This is the covenant I will make with the house of Israel after that time, declares the Lord. I will put my laws in their minds and write them on their hearts. I will be their God, and they will be my people. No longer will a man teach his neighbour, or a man his brother, saying 'Know the Lord,' because they will all know me, from the least of them to the greatest. For I will forgive their wickedness and will remember their sins no more."

Ephesians 2: 8.

"For it is by grace you have been saved, through faith – and this not from yourselves, it is the gift of God – not by works, so that no-one can boast."

1 John 4: 9–10.

"This is how God showed his love among us: He sent his one and only Son into the world that we might live through him. This is love: not that we loved God, but that he loved us and sent his Son as an atoning sacrifice for our sins. Dear friends, since God so loved us, we also should love one another."

From the Old Testament

1 Samuel 15: 22.

"Does the Lord delight in burnt offerings and sacrifices as much as in obeying the voice of the Lord? To obey is better than sacrifice, and to heed is better than the fat of rams."

Jeremiah 9: 23–24.

"This is what the Lord says: 'Let not the wise man boast of his wisdom or the strong man boast of his strength or the rich man boast of his riches, but let him who boasts boast about this: that he understands and knows me, that I am the Lord, who exercises kindness, justice and righteousness on earth, for in these I delight,' declares the Lord."

Promises mentioned in Chapter One – look up these references

that nothing can separate us from the love of God – Romans 8: 35–39

whatever we ask for he will give us – John 16: 23–24

we will have eternal life – John 11: 25–26

he will be with us always – Matthew 28: 20

he has promised us hope and a future – Jeremiah 29: 11

forgiveness and healing – Colossians 1: 13–14

freedom – John 8: 36

no condemnation – Romans 8: 1